"Testing Made Easy V2.0"

An Evaluation of Quality

"It's an inside view of what Software Testing is all about focusing on fresher's and professionals".

L.Sowmya Narayanan
Testing MindZ
03/02/2014

Table of Contents

About the Author

L.Sowmya Narayanan is a Technocrat |Entrepreneur| Academician | Testing Specialist | IT Professional | with 15 + years of experience in Software Testing.

He was instrumental in the implementation of S/W Testing Process & Templates in various companies. He has also been an Internal QA Auditor for one of the Leading IT companies in Chennai. He has travelled to the Silicon Valley & Europe towards professional engagement.

As an entrepreneur, He runs successful Software Company called 'Testing MindZ'. As a Business Builder, L.Sowmya Narayanan plays a key role in TMZ's Organization Vision, & Growth. He has been an inspiration to many of colleagues & friends.

He virtually reached millions through his blog which comprises of information on Software Testing. This blog is exclusively dedicated to software testing.

You can reach the blog at:

http://sowmyan-testinguniverse.blogspot.com

Preface of the Book

Testing Made Easy - An Evolution of Testing is a book focused on Software Testing, its scope & its approach. The Book focuses more on Manual Testing and a brief on Automation Testing. The Book is being written for all those Software Testing Professionals who are new to the testing field & to those who want to know what exactly is Software Testing is all about. It gives a complete in detail information on S/W Testing -> Process, Methods, Approach etc. It comes handy as a quick references on Software Testing.

Dedication

I dedicate this book to my family & friends. To my

S.Somasundaram (Project Manager, HLCT) through whom

I learned so much about Software Testing. To my idol Mr.

Suresh Samuel who has been a big source of inspiration

in my career. To my elder brother Mr.Raghunath

Ramaswamy who has always guided me in my career and

to all those lovely people who had been my source of

learning.

Let's Get Started

Can we imagine buying a product without a "Quality Tag"? The Quality Tag is an assurance or rather a commitment of confidence that the product will function according to its functionality.

The Advent of Testing in Software

Software Testing came into existence in 1960s, not in a structured manner but it was the beginning. The oblivious reason of the birth or rather the need for a testing came because of lack of established standards of software engineering practices.

Poor design and Regular hardware up gradation left many types of software in-effective and thus a strong need arose in the industry to produce faster and highly reliable software. The requirement of Software Testing increased with the increasing dependency on software along with good engineers.

Software Testing Originated to address the below issues:

- Enhance the processes,
- Increase the reliability of product,
- Deliver a quality product,
- Deliver in time

Introduction to Software Testing

"*Testing*" what a beautiful word to utter. A Word which brings in smile, happiness & satisfaction to all. The Word means a lot in the Real World. In the World of Software "*Successful software depends on a thorough & extremely attentive verification & validation*".

Bug Free Software

Testing is not a routine process it's a constant exploration of methods and an evolution of good ideas. To the World of Business it's a commitment a Promise to be kept every time we deliver without compromising on standards. The beauty of Quality lies in the Development & Testing of the application/product with a process of continuous learning with main focus on all aspects of the business, so that we can help the business develop the best product for our customers.

Why Testing & its Importance?

Testing should systematically uncover different classes of errors in a minimum amount of time and with a minimum amount of effort. A secondary benefit of testing is that it demonstrates that the software appears to be working as stated in the specifications. The data collected through testing can also provide an indication of the software's reliability and quality. But, testing cannot show the absence of defect -- it can only show that software defects are present.

Software Testing is Important because A Non-Tested Product results in customer Complaints and Commotions. Uncertainty & Distrust will be a strong feeling for the customers whenever they go out to buy or when using the product of that Brand. Business Owners run the huge risk of going out of business when quality and standards are not met.

What is Software Testing?

Whatis.com Defines Software Testing as "Software testing is a method of assessing the functionality of a software program"

Software testing is an investigation done to provide stakeholders with information about the quality of the product or service under test. The process of executing a program or application with the intent of finding software bugs (errors or other defects).

"Testing is the process of evaluating a system or its component(s) with the intent to find that whether it satisfies the specified requirements or not. It is a continuous process of evaluation of software in order to achieve our goals".

Testing is executing a system in order to identify any gaps, errors or missing requirements in contrary to the actual desire or requirements.

Testing assesses the quality of the product. Software testing is a verification and validation process

Attitude of a Software Tester

Attitude matters a lot for everything & particularly for S/w Tester. It reflects the way he sees the application. A tester is always a bridge between the client & company.

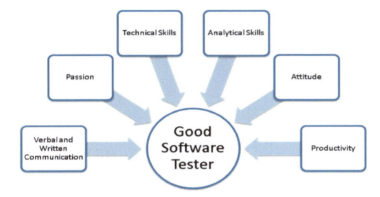

He should possess the below qualities:

- ➢ Passion for analysis & testing.

- ➢ Logical & Technical Capability.

- ➢ Flexibility.

- ➢ Communication Skills

- ➢ Business Sense.

- ➢ Constructively Destructive Sense

A Comparison on Testing with QA & QC

Quality Assurance: It is an activity where we ensure that we implement the process, procedures & Standards. We implement all these through various methods to accomplish our goals and include ensuring conformance to one or more standards, such as ISO 9000 or a model such as CMMI. It is process oriented & preventive activity and a subset of STLC.

Quality Control: It is an activity which ensures that the requirements are verified for software. The implementation of procedures and process are followed with full focus on Actual Testing. It is product oriented activity and a corrective process. It is considered as the subset of QA.

Testing: It is an activity which ensures that we identify the fallacies of the software where the focus is on actual testing. It is Product Oriented activity with a preventive process. It is a subset of Quality Control.

Methods of Testing

A testing method or a test method is a definitive procedure that produces a test result. It is a systematic approach or practice to perform a routine activity in a n ordered manner. The outcome of a test result can be a qualitative, categorical or quantities. It can be a individual observation or an output of a precision measuring instrument.

Usually the test result is the dependent on a measured value based on a particular conditions of the test and some test may involve changing of values to determine the level at which a certain result or response occurs.

Software Testing Comprises of 2 methods of testing –

- **Manual** & **Automation**

Manual testing

Testing of Software manually where in without using any automated tools or scripts an application or software is tested by the tester. In this type the tester becomes a customer inside the company meaning he takes over the role of an end user and test the Software to identify any un-expected behavior or bug. There are different stages for manual testing like unit testing, Integration testing, System testing and User Acceptance testing. Testers use test plan, test cases or test scenarios to test the Software to ensure the completeness of testing. Manual testing also includes exploratory testing as testers explore the software to identify errors in it.

Automation testing

Automation Testing means using an automation tool to execute your test case suite. Automation testing is also known as Test Automation is when the tester writes scripts and uses an Automation Tool to test the software. This process involves automation of a manual process. Automation Testing is used for test scenarios for which we need to re-run the test scenarios for multiple times.

 The Objective of Automation Testing is simplifying testing efforts and usage of Manual intervention to the minimal. The automation software can also enter test data into the System Under Test, compare expected and actual results and generate detailed test reports.

Test Automation stresses a need of considerable investments of money and resources. Successive development cycles will require execution of same test suite repeatedly. Using a test automation tool it's achievable to record this test suite and re-play it as required. Once the test suite is automated completely, we do not require any human intervention is required. This improved ROI of Test Automation.

The Automation tools are very useful to speed up the test cycle as they can replicate manual testing processes at a much faster rate.

Goal of Automation is to reduce number of test cases to be run manually and not eliminate manual testing all together. The Main Criteria or the Success Mantra automated software testing is by and large most successful when implemented by expert resource.

<u>Automated testing is important due to following reasons</u>:

- Testing of all the Workflows, Functionalities and Negative Scenarios is time consuming & also cost.
- Automation Testing is best suited for testing which requires testing the volume of data.

- It is difficult to test for multi lingual sites manually
- It's very useful for testing the performance of websites or an application.
- Automation increases speed of test execution.
- Automation helps increase Test Coverage.
- Manual Testing is error prone as it's a repeated activity involving human intervention.

What can we automate?

Automation is best suited for the following criterion to increase the automation ROI

- Critical Business Requirements which are of High Risk.
- Repeated Execution of Test Cases
- Test Cases that is very monotonous or difficult to perform manually.
- Test Cases which are lengthy.

What we cannot automate?

- ❖ Applications or Software which are having Frequent Changing Requirements.
- ❖ A newly designed application and is not tested manually (at least once).
- ❖ Adhoc Testing (or) Random Testing.

Software Automation Testing Tools

Automation Testing Tools is used mostly used for two important areas for an application. One to test their functionality and another to test the load/ performance of the application/websites or software.

Automation Testing Tools available in the Market

Tool Purpose	Tool Name	Company
Functional	QTP(Quick Test Professional)	HP
Functional	Win Runner	
Performance/Load	Load Runner	HP
Performance	Silk Performer	Borland
Load	QA Load	Compuware

What is COQ "The Cost of Quality"?

"*Every time work is redone, the cost of quality increases*".

The "cost of quality" is not the price of creating a quality product or service. It's the cost of NOT creating a quality product or service. It does not include costs associated with maintenance and quality training.

Examples include:

• The reworking of a manufactured item.

• The retesting of an assembly.

• The rebuilding of a tool.

• The correction of a bank statement.

• The reworking of a service, such as the reprocessing of a loan operation or the replacement of a food order in a restaurant.

In short, any cost that would not have been expended if quality were perfect contributes to the cost of quality.

The Total Quality Costs are the total of the cost incurred by:

• Investing in the prevention of nonconformance to requirements.

• Appraising a product or service for conformance to requirements.

• Failing to meet requirements.

Software Metrics

It is a mechanism to know the effectiveness of the testing that can be measured quantitatively. It is a feedback mechanism to improve the Testing Process that is followed currently. Testing metric is used to track actual testing progress against plan and therefore to be able to be proactive upon early indications that testing activity is falling behind. The objective of Test Metrics is to capture the planned and actual quantities the effort, time and resources required to complete all the phases of Testing of the SW Project. Metrics are the numerical data, which will help us to measure the test effectiveness. There are several test metrics identified as part of the overall testing activity in order to track and measure the entire testing process.

These test metrics are collected at each phase of the testing life cycle /SDLC and analyzed and appropriate process improvements are determined and implemented as a result of these test metrics that are constantly collected and evaluated as a parallel activity together with testing both for manual and automated testing irrespective of the type of application.

The test metrics can be broadly classified into the following three categories such as:

- *Project Related Metrics*
- *Process Related Metrics*
- *Customer Related Metrics*

Project Related Metrics –> such as Test Size,# of Test Cases tested per day –Automated (NTTA),# of Test Cases tested per day –Manual (NTTM),# of Test Cases created per day – Manual (TCED),Total number of review defects (RD), Total number of testing defects (TD), etc

Process Related Metrics –> such as Schedule Adherence (SA), Effort Variance (EV), Schedule Slippage (SS), Test Cases and Scripts Rework Effort, etc.

Customer related Metrics –> such as Percentage of defects leaked per release (PDLPR), Percentage of automation per release (PAPR), Application Stability Index (ASI), etc.

Basics Test Metrics that are used to measure testing some of them are listed below:

- **Effort** (HM) = productivity(Hour-men/FP) * size (FP) FP means Functional Points.

For Example: Effort = (Productivity * total afp)/ 21 *8 (Here 21 is the no: of working days & 8 (is the number of working hrs per day) so the total effort comes to = (12 * 400) / (21*8) = 28.57 man months~= 29 man months. 12 is a random figure in hrs. Now assuming your average man month cost is 1 lakh, so the total cost of developing the software comes to 29 *1 = 29 lakhs

- **To Calculate Man Days** = Total Effort/8
- **To Calculate Man Months** = Man Days * 22 days. (No.of.days depends on the company)

- To Calculate Productivity (test cases executed per day) = Effort /Size.

- **Rework Effort Ratio**:{(Actual rework efforts spent in that phase / Total actual efforts spent in that phase)} * 100

- **Test Case Adequacy**: This defines the number of actual test cases created vs. estimated test cases at the end of test case preparation phase.

  It is calculated as->   No. of actual test cases / No: of test cases estimated

- **Test Case Effectiveness**: This defines the effectiveness of test cases which is measured in number of defects found in testing without using the test cases.

  It is calculated as :-> No. of defects detected using test cases*100/Total no: of defects detected

- **Effort Variance** : {(Actual Efforts-Estimated Efforts) / Estimated Efforts} *100

- **Schedule Variance**:{(Actual Duration - Estimated Duration)/Estimated Duration} *1

What is Scope of Testing?

A Scope of Testing is where we define what to test and what not to test. It clearly defines our area of testing the application or system. Unless we are clear with our scope or area of testing it is not advisable to start our testing. The testing team describes specifically what you want to accomplish by identifying what you will test and what you will not.

For example, you might limit your testing of client computer hardware to the minimum supported configurations or to the standard configurations.

When Should Testing Occur?

Testing is a continuous process which has to be performed at every stage of development to bring out a quality product. Testing is performed after coding/development phase is done for a product. Test data sets must be derived and their correctness and consistency should be monitored throughout the development process. If testing is isolated as a single phase late in the cycle, errors in the problem statement or design may incur costs. Therefore, testing should not be isolated as an inspection activity. Rather testing should be involved throughout the SDLC in order to bring out a quality product.

Software Test Life Cycle (STLC)

A process which is executed in systematic and planned manner. Different activities are carried out to improve the quality of the product. Each Activity is carried out in a planned & systematic manner. Every phase of STLC has a specific goal & deliverables. It defines the stages or steps that are followed in testing software or an application. It's a Step by step approach of testing. It is part of Software Development Lifecycle (SDLC), a subset of testing.

Software Test Life Cycle

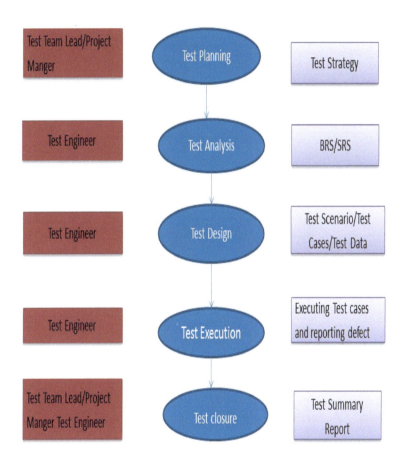

Phase	Activity	Deliverables
Requirements Analysis	You review the software requirements	▪ System description ▪ Resources ▪ Deliverables schedule ▪ Business Need ▪ Cost-Benefit Analysis
Test Planning	Once you have gathered a general idea of what needs to be tested, you 'plan' for the tests.	▪ Test Plan ▪ Test Estimation ▪ Test Schedule
Test Analysis	You analyze on what testing needs to be done. If any automation is to be done. We decide in this phase on what we will automate & how will you automate them. Non Testing Areas are also defined in this phase.	
Test Designing	You design/detail your tests on the basis of detailed requirements/design of the software (sometimes, on the basis of your imagination).	▪ Test Cases /Test Data ▪ Requirements Traceability Matrix

Test Execution	You execute your Test Cases/Scripts in the Test Environment to see whether they pass.	▪ Test Results (Incremental) ▪ Defect Reports
Test Reporting	You prepare various reports for various stakeholders.	▪ Test Results (Final) ▪ Test/Defect Metrics ▪ Test Closure Report.

Levels of Testing

Testing has always an activity of V&V where in we continue to verify & validate the results and ensure that the application is working according to the requirements. In order to perform this testing has been introduced to enhance a unified approach towards testing activities and also to ensure that this unified approach & methodology is used & is made available across several different projects. This classification of testing process clearly indicates that a mutiple tests can be performed simulatenously.

The levels of testing have a hierarchical structure which starts building from through the bottom-up approach where higher levels assume successful and satisfactory completion of lower level tests.

Without this structured approach, would be a very difficult task. It is normally required for unit testing to be done before integration testing which is done before system testing and acceptance testing. Each level of test is characterized by an environment i.e. a type of people, hardware, software, data and interface

There are four levels of software testing:

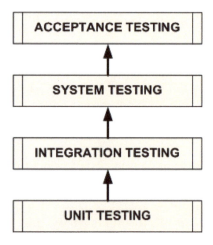

1. <u>**Unit Testing**</u> is a level of the software testing process where individual units/components of a software/system are tested. The purpose is to

validate that each unit of the software performs as designed.

2. **Integration Testing** is a level of the software testing process where individual units are combined and tested as a group. The purpose of this level of testing is to expose faults in the interaction between integrated units.

3. **System Testing** is a level of the software testing process where a complete, integrated system/software is tested. The purpose of this test is to evaluate the system's compliance with the specified requirements.

4. **Acceptance Testing** is a level of the software testing process where a system is tested for acceptability. The purpose of this test is to evaluate the system's compliance with the business requirements and assess whether it is acceptable for delivery.

Test Deliverables

There are different test deliverables at every phase of the SDLC. These deliverables are provided based on the requirement once before the start of the test phase and there are other deliverables that are produced towards the end/after completion of each test phase. Also there are several test metrics that are collected at each phase of testing.

__The various test deliverables corresponding to each test phase along with their test metrics__:

- **Test Trace-ability Matrix**
- **Test Plan**
- **Testing Strategy**
- **Test Cases (for functional testing)**
- **Test Scenarios (for non-functional testing)**
- **Test Scripts**
- **Test Data**
- **Test Results**
- **Test Summary Report**
- **Release Notes**
- **Tested Build**
- **Test Metrics** (*for each level of testing not restricting to one level*).

Introduction to Test Planning

A Test Plan is a document which defines the systematic approach of execution of testing and step by step approach of activities of testing. The Test Plan contains a detailed understanding of the eventual workflow of testing.

Definition of Test Plan:

According to TMMI

"The purpose of Test Planning is to define a test approach based on the identified risks and the defined test strategy, and to establish and maintain well-founded plans for performing and managing the testing activities".

The plans are to be prepared by Test/QA Leads or by Project Managers only. In all test plans, the ETVX {Entry-Task-Validation-Exit} criteria are to be mentioned. Entry means the entry point to that phase. For example, for unit testing, the coding must be complete and then only one can start unit testing. Task is the activity that is performed.

Validation is the way in which the progress and correctness and compliance are verified for that phase. Exit tells the completion criteria of that phase, after the validation is done. For example, the exit criterion for unit testing is all unit test cases must pass.

ETVX is a modeling technique for developing worldly and atomic level models. It stands for Entry, Task, Verification and Exit. It is a task-based model where the details of each task are explicitly defined in a specification table against each phase i.e. Entry, Exit, Task, Feedback In, Feedback Out, and measures.

Contents of a Test Plan

A sample Test Plan Outline along with their description is as shown below:

Test Plan Outline

1. Definition /Test Objectives
2. Roles and Responsibilities
3. Levels of Testing & Test Strategy
4. Test Approach
5. What Test to be done & What not to tested
6. Testing Requirements
7. Resources
8. Testing Schedule
9. Assumptions and Risks

    a. **Assumptions**

    b. **Risks**

10. Testing Coverage

11. Sign-off and Acknowledgement

Definition /Test Objective: The overall purpose of testing is to ensure the {name of application} application performs at an acceptable level for the customer.

Roles & Responsibilities: It defines the roles to be played by each individual for a Test Deliverables.

Resource Type	Responsibilities	Name
Quality Manager	▪ Be the main source of Communication and agree upon on the format and scope of UAT with the customers. ▪ Agreement of acceptance criteria with the customer prior to commencing UAT. ▪ Ensure that a detailed test plan is available for test users	
Business Analyst	▪ Assist Quality Manager with the creation of a detailed test plan ▪ Ensure that bugs identified during UAT are logged into Bug Tracking Tool ▪ Ensure testing takes place within agreed timeframes. ▪ Execute test scripts/cases to ensure the application performs at an acceptable level. ▪ Document testing results.	

Levels of Testing : The Levels of Testing includes various of testing that are planned to be performed and how many rounds of these levels of testing is going to performed will be discussed in this area.

Test Strategy: It describes the outline of the testing approach that is going to be followed to achieve the goal.

"Most Companies include Test Approach" or "Strategy" inside the Test Plan, which is fine and it is usually the case for small projects. However, for larger projects, there is one Test Strategy document and different number of Test Plans for each phase or level of testing Strategy".

Test Approach: The test approach describes the types of tests performed and the sequence of tests as executed in the testing activiites.

Testing Requirements: Testing will take place in <insert location>. Some Test Engineers may choose to perform some testing from their regular workstations where it is possible. Test results must still be coordinated with others.

- Testing will take place beginning on < insert date>.

- Identified testing participants will receive instructions prior to the start of testing.

- Identified testing participants will perform the equivalent of their normal business function in the upgraded environment.

- Test scripts/cases and scenarios will be prepared prior to the start of Testing.

- Test participants will conduct the tests and document results.

- Defects will be entered into Bug Tracking Tool and tracked by the Testers.

Resources: Resources should include representatives from all areas involved in the application. It will be good that we include representatives from across the systems as it benefits us in validating the systems functions before the upgrade goes live in production.

Resource Name	Department/Area Representing	Area of Testing Focus

Test Schedule: A test schedule includes the testing steps or tasks, the target start and end dates, and responsibilities. It should also describe how the test will be reviewed, tracked, and approved.

Activity	Lead Responsibility	Date
Identify and select testers for Testing	QA Manager	
Develop test scenarios and scripts/cases	Business Analyst	
Validate participants availability for testing	QA Manager	
Review scenarios/scripts for accuracy, completeness and sequence (confirm test data is correct)	QA Manager/Senior BA's/ PM	
Ensure Testing configuration for testing activities	BA's	
Testing environment validation	Business Analyst	
Testing by Testing participants	QA Manager/Senior BA's	

Assumptions & Risks:

Assumptions: It discuss the post-planning method that deal with uncertainty. It is used to identify the most important assumptions in a testing and to accommodate unexpected outcomes.

Risks: It discusses the Risks that may arise while doing analyze & testing of the software and the ways to mitigate the same.

Risks in the project involves

- ❖ Budget Risk
- ❖ Operational Risk
- ❖ Technical Risk
- ❖ Programmatic Risk.

Test Coverage: This area of the test plan discusses the features of the software that are to be tested & not tested.

Signoff & Acknowledgment: It discusses the acceptance of the Testing Activities by Senior Members of Testing Group for that project along with their signatures for the successful implementation of the Software.

What is a Test Case & how to build it?

A Test Case is a step by step approach to achieve the expected result. Designing good test cases is a complex art. The complexity comes from three sources they are as below:

- Test cases help us discover information. Different types of tests are more effective for different classes of information.

- Test cases can be "good" in a variety of ways. No test case will be good in all of them.

- People tend to create test cases according to certain testing styles, such as domain testing or risk-based testing. Good domain tests are different from good risk-based tests

What's a scenario?

A scenario is a hypothetical story, used to help a person think through a complex problem or system.

A test case describes a set of actions to be performed and the results that are expected. A test case should target specific functionality or aim to exercise a valid path through a use case. This should include invalid user actions and illegal inputs that are not necessarily listed in the use case. A test case is described depends on several factors, e.g. the number of test cases, the frequency with which they change, the level of automation employed, the skill of the testers, the selected testing methodology, staff turnover, and risk.

The test cases will have a generic format as below

TC ID	TC Desc	Test Pre-Requisite	Test Steps	Expected Result	Actual Result	Pass /Fail	Date & Remarks

Description of the above contents

Test case ID - The test case id must be unique across the application.

Test case description - The test case description must be very brief.

Test prerequisite - The test pre-requisite clearly describes what should be present in the system, before the test can be executes.

"Testing Made Easy V2.0"

Test Inputs - The test input is nothing but the test data that is prepared to be fed to the system.

Test steps - The test steps are the step-by-step instructions on how to carry out the test.

Expected Results - The expected results are the ones that say what the system must give as output or how the system must react based on the test steps.

Actual Results – The actual results are the ones that say outputs of the action for the given inputs or how the system reacts for the given inputs.

Pass/Fail - If the Expected and Actual results are same then test is Pass otherwise Fail.

For example, In the Online shopping application, If the user enters valid Email id and Username values, let us assume that Design document says, that the system must display a product details and should insert the Email id and Username in database table. If user enters invalid values the system will display appropriate error message and will

not store it in database.

A Login Screen

Test Conditions for the fields in the Login screen

Email-It should be in this format (For E.g. clickme@yahoo.com).

Username – It should accept only alphabets not greater than 6.Numerics and special type of characters are not allowed.

Test Prerequisite - The user should have access to Customer Login screen form screen

Negative Test Case

Project Name- Online shopping. Version-1.2. Module-Catalog

ID	Description	Test Inputs	Expected Results	Actual results	Pass/ Fail
1	Check for inputting values in Email field	Email=lsowmya@hotmail.com Username=Xavier	Inputs should not be accepted. It should display message "Enter valid Email"		
2	Check for inputting values in Email field	Email=john26#rediffmail.com Username=John	Inputs should not be accepted. It should display message "Enter valid Email"		
3	Check for inputting values in Username field	Email=shilpa@yahoo.com Username=Mark24	Inputs should not be accepted. It should display message "Enter correct Username"		

Positive Test Case

Project Name- Online shopping. Version-1.2. Module-Catalog

ID	Description	Test Inputs	Expected Results	Actual results	Pass/Fail
1	Check for inputting values in Email field	Email=shan@ya hoo.com Username =dave	Inputs should be accepted.		
2	Check for inputting values in Email field	Email =knki@rediffmai l.com Username =john	Inputs should be accepted.		
3	Check for inputting values in Username field	Email=xav@yah oo.com Username=mark	Inputs should be accepted.		

How to do Test execution?

Test execution means the actual testing activities, all activities necessary to assess the results of testing and to be able to fix the identified problems. It includes the execution of test cases or test scripts, manually or in an automated way, the logging of test results, comparison of the expected and actual results, reporting the incidents and retesting the fixed bugs.

What is Test Reporting?

The test report is the final presentation of the test results and is a tool for determining the success of the Testing. It is usually the only lasting credible source of information for what occurred during a test program. The main objective of a test report is to address the performance of a system and to recommend standard of improvements. The execution of testing should be recorded in the test results and using them test reports is collected as proof of the activities that are executed.

The test report should:

• Test Summary,

• Failed Tests

- Recommendations and finally Signatures of the Respective Departments Heads who are involved in this Project.

Template of a Project Report Document

Template of
Project Report Document

1. Test Summary

This test was run by _____<your name> on _____ (date) in using a _____ (platform type) for Build Number _____.

Total Number of Test Cases	Total Executed Passed	Total Pass	Total Fail

2. Failure Summary Table

The following table list the failed tests noted in the Test Summary.

Test Step #	Business Scenarios	Priority/Severity	Description of Failure

3. Recommendations

Based on the above results we recommend from the Quality Assurance

Department _____ (Acceptance/Rejection) of this product.

Name	Signature	Date
_____	_____	_____
_____	_____	_____
_____	_____	_____

What is a Defect?

A *software defect* is a deficiency in a software product that causes it to perform unexpectedly. From a software user's perspective, a defect is anything that causes the software not to meet their expectations. In this context, a *software user* can be either a person or another piece of software.

It is basically the Variation that arises from the actual result to the expected result while executing the test cases is known as defects. Different organizations have different names to describe this variation, commonly defects are also known as bug, problem, incidents or issues. We log these incidents just to keep track of the record of what is observed during the testing so that we can find out the solution to correct it.

A defect in software results from some type of mistake. Usually these mistakes are a result of human error, but sometimes they are caused by systemic errors in the development process. Mistakes can also result from faulty development tools, a misunderstanding of customer requirements, or other issues that arise in the course of software development.

Fortunately, not every mistake leads to a defect, but almost all defects can be traced back to some type of mistake.

Bug / Fault / Error: -

The single focus for any tester is to find a bug/error or an issue in an application. In order to ensure that the application behaves or performs according to the required result.

So, what exactly these bugs & errors are:

- **Error:** A discrepancy between a computed, observed, or measured value or condition and the true, specified, or theoretically correct value or condition

- **Failure:** The inability of a system or component to perform its required functions within specified performance requirements.

- **Bug:** A fault in a program which causes the program to perform in an unintended or unanticipated manner.

- **Fault:** An incorrect step, process, or data definition in a computer program which causes the program to perform in an unintended or unanticipated manner.

- **Defect**: Commonly refers to several troubles with the software products, with its external behavior or with its internal features

But as for a test engineer all are same as the above definition is only for the purpose of documentation or indicative.

What is a Defect Management?

Defects determine the effectiveness of what Testing we do. Defect management is an integral part of a development and test process in many software development organizations. It is a sub-process of the development process.

Sub-Process of the development process is the following:

- *defect prevention,*
- *discovery,*
- *recording & reporting,*
- *classification, resolution, prediction*

An insight of Bug Tracking System

A bug tracking system is a software application that is designed to help quality assurance and programmers keep track of reported software bugs in their work. It may be regarded as a sort of issue tracking system. Typically bug tracking systems are integrated with other software project management applications. Having a bug tracking system is extremely valuable in software development, and they are used extensively by companies developing software products.

How to record the bugs?

While testing an application/software you will encounter various challenges & it is important you report them & keep records of your findings. Because these are vital information which gives more clarity towards a better quality delivers.

When reporting a bug in a Test Management Tool or in an Excel sheet as used by the company:

- **Heading** – Heading should be short & clear.

- **Details of the bug** – Specify Which Environment, Build Version, Priority & Severity of the bug, DB, Backend Details.

- **Subject of the Bug** – In the Subject please give details like Description of the bug & Steps to be reproduced. Please also include the test data used when error occurred.

- **Screen shot** – During execution of testing when an error/bug occurs kindly take a screenshot of the same using the "*PrintScr*" button of the Keyboard or using the Snipping Tool take the screenshot along with the date & time as this will help the developer to analyze the issue better.

Life Cycle of a Bug:

Bug life cycles are similar to software development life cycles. At any time during the software development life cycle errors can be made during the gathering of requirements, requirements analysis, functional design, internal design, documentation planning, document preparation, coding, unit testing, test planning, integration, testing, maintenance, updates, re-testing and phase-out.

Bug life cycle begins when a programmer, software developer, or architect makes a mistake, creates an unintentional software defect, i.e. bug, and ends when the bug is fixed, and the bug is no longer in existence.

What should be done after a bug is found?

When a bug is found, it needs to be communicated and assigned to developers that can fix it. After the problem is resolved, fixes should be re-tested. Additionally, determinations should be made regarding requirements, software, hardware, safety impact, etc., for regression testing to check the fixes didn't create other problems elsewhere. If a problem-tracking system is in place, it should encapsulate these determinations. A variety of commercial, problem-tracking, management software tools are available. These tools, with the detailed input of software test engineers, will give the team complete information so developers can understand the bug, get an idea of its severity, reproduce it and fix it. In software development process, the bug has a life cycle. The bug should go through the life cycle to be closed. A specific life cycle ensures that the process is standardized. The bug attains different states in the life cycle.

The life cycle of the bug can be shown diagrammatically as follows:

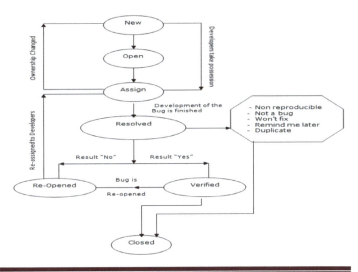

The different states of a bug can be summarized as follows:

1. New
2. Open
3. Assign
4. Resolved
5. Non-Reproducible
6. Not a Bug
7. Won't Fix
8. Remind me Later
9. Reopened
10. Duplicate
11. Verified
12. Closed

Description of Various Stages:

1. New: When the bug is posted for the first time, its state will be "NEW". This means that the bug is not yet approved.

2. Open: After a tester has posted a bug, the lead of the tester approves that the bug is genuine and he changes the state as "OPEN".

3. Assign: Once the lead changes the state as "OPEN", he assigns the bug to corresponding developer or developer team. The state of the bug now is changed to "ASSIGN".

4. Resolved: Once the developer fixes the bug, he has to assign the bug to the testing team for next round of testing. Before he releases the software with bug fixed, he changes the state of bug to "Resolved". It specifies that the bug has been fixed and is released to testing team.

5. Non – Reproducible: When bug is not getting reproduced in the developer environment at this stage this state is affected. The scenarios can be like when the functionality of the application where bug was reported is not getting reproduced.

6. Won't Fix: The bug, changed to Won't Fix state means the bug is expected to be fixed in next releases. The reasons for changing the bug to this state are priority of the bug may be low; lack of time for the release or the bug may not have major effect on the software.

7. Not a Bug: If the developer feels that the bug is not genuine, he rejects the bug. Then the state of the bug is changed to "Not a Bug".

8. Duplicate: If the bug is repeated twice or the two bugs mention the same concept of the bug, then one bug status is changed to "DUPLICATE".

9. Remind me Later : If the developer feels he is not having the time to fix the issue or if he needs to fix the issue only in the next release because of various factors some of them may be in the change of functionality of the application at that time this state is being used

10. Verified: Once the bug is fixed and the status is changed to "RESOLVED", the tester tests the bug. If the bug is not present in the software, he approves that the bug is fixed and changes the status to "VERIFIED".

11. Reopened: If the bug still exists even after the bug is fixed by the developer, the tester changes the status to "REOPENED". The bug traverses the life cycle once again.

12. Closed: Once the bug is fixed, it is tested by the tester. If the tester feels that the bug no longer exists in the software, he changes the status of the bug to "CLOSED". This state means that the bug is fixed, tested and approved.

While defect prevention is much more effective and efficient in reducing the number of defects, most organization conducts defect discovery and removal. Discovering and removing defects is an expensive and inefficient process. It is much more efficient for an organization to conduct activities that prevent defects.

Guidelines on deciding the Severity of Bug:

Indicate the **impact** each defect has on **testing efforts** or users and administrators of the application under test. This information is used by developers and management as the **basis** for assigning **priority** of work on defects.

A guideline for assignment of Priority Levels during the product/project test phase includes:

1. Critical / Show Stopper — An item that prevents further testing of the product or function under test can be classified as Critical Bug. No workaround is possible for such bugs.

Examples of this include a missing menu option or security permission required to access a function under test.

2. **Major / High** — A defect that does not function as expected/designed or cause other functionality to fail to meet requirements can be classified as Major Bug. The workaround can be provided for such bugs. Examples of this include inaccurate calculations; the wrong field being updated, etc.

3. **Average / Medium** — The defects which do not conform to standards and conventions can be classified as Medium Bugs. Easy workarounds exists to achieve functionality objectives. Examples include matching visual and text links which lead to different end points.

4. **Minor / Low** — Cosmetic defects which does not affect the functionality of the system can be classified as Minor Bugs.

When is Testing to be stopped? "Push the Stop Button"!!!!

- Testing should be stopped when it meets the completion criteria. Now how to find the completion criteria?

- **Completion criteria** can be derived from test plan and test strategy document. Also, re-check your test coverage.

- Completion criteria should be based on Risks.

Testing should be stopped when -

❖ Test cases completed with certain percentage passed and test coverage is achieved.

❖ There are no known critical bugs.

❖ Coverage of code, functionality, or requirements reaches a specified point

❖ Bug rate falls below a certain level, now testers are not getting any priority 1, 2, or 3 bugs.

As testing is a never ending process we can never assume that 100 % testing has been done, we can only minimize the risk of shipping the product to client with X testing done.

Latest Trends of Software Testing

In this section we are going to brief about what are the various areas or sources we can look out for the future of testing. The Various Technology and Industry to look out for. The growth of ecommerce is getting bigger & bigger. The usage of internet has become the integral part of our life. The Customers demand & expectation is going to be bigger.

> ➤ **Social Networking:** Sites will play a huge role in the coming areas. So many Data's of individual's means maintenance of the data. Data Warehousing & Data Testing will play a very key role in the second half more from 2014. Expect a Boom.

> ➤ **Client Side Performance:** Considering the huge success of powerful JavaScript libraries and the integration of third party apps, the client side performance will suffer. So the focus will be on testing the browser performance impression in combination to the server performance.

- ➤ **Mobile Performance**: Standard performance tests will be extended to mobile sites covering bandwidth as well as client site issues.

- ➤ **Automated Cross-Browser Testing**: In a perfect world, every site behaves the same, no matter which browser is used. But we do not live in a perfect word. So not only test automation is important, but being able to perform them on different platforms running different browsers.

- ➤ **Mobile Application Development**: There is a boom in the telecommunication world our cell phones are replaced by smart phones to our data. Now we have our world in our palm. There is a lot of scope of testing involves the lot of testing, applications across the wide range of handset and the languages there are different careers, carriers or manufacturers and then the locations to take care of.

- ➤ **TaaS (Testing as a Service)/Cloud testing** :Testing as a Service (TaaS) is an outsourcing model in which testing activities associated with some of an organization's business activities are performed by a service provider rather than employees. *TaaS* is most suitable for specialized testing efforts that don't require a lot of in-depth knowledge of the design or the system.

➢ **TDD (Test Driven Development)**: Test driven development known as TDD, was discovered by Kent Beck in 2003 it is not exactly a new technique but it is gaining importance. It ensures that the source code is thoroughly unit tested as many of us are aware that unit testing is not always done.

➢ **Crowd Sourcing**: Crowd sourcing that is another emerging that is catching up. Crowd sourcing is a combination of the words crowd and outsourcing, this is coined by Jeff Howe in June 2006. It is a new approach wherein a group of people or individual volunteer to test the application like a free tester can login to the site can specifically call or asks tester and known the objective of testing. Crowd source testing companies provide the platform for the testing cycle to crowd source a product to a community of testers who register for the testing service voluntarily. The testers are paid per bug depending on the type of bug and its market price. Obviously Critical Bugs are paid high.

➤ **Security**: Security testing again this is the cloud and net applications. The purpose of the security testing is to discover the vulnerabilities of a web application, so the developers can remove the vulnerability or the glitch form application and make the web application and data safe from unauthorized actions or hackers.

The Grand Finale

Every Good thing has to come to an end so is this Book. But every end there is a new beginning, new horizon of hope. To Sum up of what we glanced across through all those pages in the book. Testing has come a long way from where it has started with "Quality" taking a pivotal role in the products and it is the mantra of the hour. Quality has paved in as a catalyst of growth and prosperity to the world. Product Developer & Business Owners focus on Quality driven Delivery & Serve better. With the world moving towards new technology like cloud computing, web application, smart phones, online shopping, Ecommerce, Online Banking with stricter regulations have given rise to a whole new world of testing. The usage of internet has become the integral part of our life with the Customers demand & expectation growing bigger. So, we cannot imagine a world without Quality. So, the word *"Testing & Quality" is not only beautiful but also holds importance for our very existence"*

Happy Testing

Testing Rocks!!!

www.ingramcontent.com/pod-product-compliance
Lightning Source LLC
Chambersburg PA
CBHW041144050326
40689CB00001B/483